Thanksgiving Pie for the Animals

How an Apple Pie for Thanksgiving Led to a Fall Feast for the Wild Critters!

By
Susie Binkley

In memory of my Dad,
Raymond Voige
Who filled bird feeders with me when I was a child and eventually handed me his camera and said, "Now you try!"

ISBN 1456314815
EAN-13 9781456314811

Printed in the United States of America

To contact the author please send an email to:
susiebinkleybooks@gmail.com

The Story of Thanksgiving Pie for the Animals

We had been feeding the wild animals around our yard for years. Then one Thanksgiving we were peeling apples for pie early in the morning, when one of our critter feeder "regulars" stopped by looking for her breakfast. Lottie the squirrel, who'd been coming to our house for peanuts, cracked corn and sunflower seeds since she was a tiny baby, was on our deck staring in the window at the table full of apples. She stood up and looked at me, curling in her little golden hands, and waited. I looked at the apple I was peeling in my hand, and the plate of cores and peels in front of me.

"Oh! Do you want this?" I asked her, giggling. I opened the sliding door and set an apple core gently on the deck. Lottie wasted no time retrieving my gift. She snatched it up and jumped up on the deck rail. The family all gathered around laughing as Lottie nibbled away at the apple core like a kid eating corn on the cob! She turned it and turned it as she nibbled, making her way all around and down the core till it was completely clean. She dropped it, licked her paws and looked at me again as if to say "More, please!!!" Not wanting to over-stuff her, this time I offered a piece of peel and a couple of peanuts. Once again she popped up on to the rail and put on quite a show. The nut shells flew everywhere and the peel disappeared in a hurry!

Who you're seeing: On each pair of pages in this book, you'll see a "who you're seeing" section with details about the kinds of critters you're seeing and/or what's going on in the pictures. (This page) Lottie the Fox Squirrel on our deck rail. (Opposite, Top) Lottie on our steps "begging"! (Opposite, bottom left) A Eurasian Collared Dove. (Opposite, bottom right) A Black-billed Magpie.

Lottie's sweet personality and funny antics are why I began photographing backyard wildlife!

I glanced down next to the deck, to the spot where I feed the birds and critters. Muffin and Pumpkin (two bunnies) were there, as well as some little birds and a Magpie, chowing down on the seed I'd placed out that morning. I looked at my daughter, who was peeling apples, too, and smiled. "You know," I said, "*we're* having an apple pie, so why shouldn't *they*?" I nodded out the window at all our wild friends. My daughter squealed with delight and began listing all the ingredients we could include in *their* pie.

And so began the tradition of Thanksgiving Pie for the Animals

Over the years we've gotten more elaborate in our offerings, but that first year it was just a paper plate with seeds, peanuts, apple cores and peels.

As the years went by more people heard about our tradition and just loved it. So I decided to hone my wildlife photography skills and create a book that would inspire others to include *their wild friends* in their day of thanks as well.

I know how thankful I am for the beauty, grace and joy they bring to my life. And the fun!

Who you're seeing: (This page) Lottie the Fox Squirrel eating a peanut from the first Thanksgiving pie. (Opposite, bottom) A Mountain Cottontail deciding what to eat first!

This year's pictures are much fancier, but our first
Thanksgiving pie was just as special!

Turn the page to see how this one small "pie" on a paper plate inspired us to
create a fall feast for our wild friends. And to see just how fancy this
celebration became!

I wanted this book to be pretty to look at, funny to read, and somewhat whimsical! So I decided to "set a fancy table" for the animals, just as we do for ourselves on Thanksgiving! I chose a colorful tablecloth and some pretty dishes, and my daughter and I spent a few days planning how to make some interesting "pies" to serve. Eventually we chose to use four kinds of birdseed mix, cracked corn, raisins, peanut butter and apples- some from our own tree! Over a month of picture-taking, the pies were re-made many times!

For one pie, we made concentric rings of raisins, seeds, and corn, topped off with a whole apple.

For the other we used the peanut butter to form the center of a "flower" made of apple peels.

The whole family helped build the picture-taking "scene". We put up some fall décor, a few colorful mums, and some cute plates shaped like leaves. I covered a small table with a waterproof tablecloth and waited to see if the animals would take to it! But they soon let me know something was unacceptable!

For five years these animals had been coming to our yard and eating off of an old glass patio table- a makeshift "platform feeder". These are used for ground-feeding birds that don't like hanging feeders. I soon found many critters hanging out on the old glass table I'd pushed near the kids' swing set, as if they were waiting for their food to arrive over there! I finally gave in and brought the table in to the scene, after Drake the Fox Squirrel (below) kept begging, even though the glare from the glass was a real challenge to work with photographically!

Who you're seeing: A Fox Squirrel waiting on the glass table. Isn't it funny how humans and animals have "habits" we get in to! We're much more alike than we think!

(Bottom, left) The original scene did not contain the glass table!

This is it!
The table is set for
Thanksgiving Pie for the Animals!

Our story begins...

Hey my little friends!

We're in here giving thanks for all the wonderful things in our lives, and we're having a special feast to celebrate!

This year we've decided to share our feast with you, because we're so thankful for the beauty and joy you bring to our lives.

So enjoy this feast! And while you do...won't you please tell us what you're all thankful for?

Happy Thanksgiving!

"Wow! Look at that buffet!"

"Is this for US?"

Who you're seeing: (This page) A Western Scrub-jay and a Mountain Cottontail. It sure didn't take the animals long to figure out that something was new! (Opposite) A Fox Squirrel looks very curious.

"That's what she said!"

"This is amazing!"

"Wow! They even set out fancy dishes!"

"And pretty decor!"

Who you're seeing: (Opposite) A Black-billed Magpie on the glass table, a Western Scrub-jay in flight, and a Mountain Cottontail. (This page) Another Mountain Cottontail and Western Scrub-jay helping themselves to a meal.

"You mean *yummy* décor!"

"Oh Pumpkin! Why are you eating the décor?"

"Why does someone always do something embarrassing at the holidays!?"

Who you're seeing: Pumpkin the Mountain Cottontail (both pages) and one of her kits (left, looking embarrassed). She's lived under our deck and around our yard for four years! Her favorite "dish" at the buffet definitely turned out to be the mums! She nibbled the yellow and purple flowers down to nothing. Rabbits are known for being destructive in gardens. I guess she's no exception. She's still adorable! Even if she mowed the mums.

"It's just so good!"

"I'm digging in!"

"Why it looks wonderful!"

"How nice of them!"

Who you're seeing: (Opposite) A Fox Squirrel wasting no time digging in! (This page) A Pine Siskin on a sock feeder and a Mountain Chickadee in a gate! Both birds are small compared to other birds often seen with them, such as American Goldfinches or Black-capped Chickadees. They are, however, larger than the Lesser Goldfinches you'll see in these pages. They're truly tiny!

"So how does it taste?"

Who you're seeing (This page, top) Three Lesser Goldfinches. They often hang on the sock feeder in groups and eat Niger seed. (This page, bottom) a Mountain Cottontail and a Western Scrub-jay are the first to come test the pie. Look how well they're sharing. What nice manners for a "Thanksgiving" feast! (Opposite) A Western Scrub-jay and a Fox Squirrel.

"This is SO good!"

"We've got to go tell our families and friends!"

"We can help tell everyone! Because what we're thankful for...
Is the chance to *soar*..."

"When life gives you wings... *fly!*"

Who you're seeing: (Opposite, above) A Black-billed Magpie. Magpies are stunningly beautiful in flight, especially when the sun is shining through their feathers! (Opposite, below) a Red-tailed Hawk. They are easy to identify by the flash of red on the top of their tails. (This page, top) a male Red-winged Blackbird. Nothing beats the bright display of their red shoulder patches in flight. When flocking in fall and winter, it creates quite a show! This page, center) A female Lesser Goldfinch coming in for a landing. (This page, bottom) a Western Scrub-jay. Their iridescent feathers flash in the sunlight.

"Thank you for inviting us!"   "Now we're thankful ..."

"For having so many wonderful choices in life!!!"

Who you're seeing: (Opposite, top) A Western Scrub-jay, (opposite, bottom) a Fox Squirrel trying to choose! (This page) a Mountain Cottontail. They appreciate all the choices at their buffet... do you appreciate all the many choices you have in life? Consider making one of your choices to spend time out in nature, having some fun and getting to know your wild friends!

"And for friends who are nice enough to share..."

Who you're seeing: (Opposite, top) Lesser Goldfinches eating Niger seed from a sock feeder. (Opposite, bottom) A Mountain Cottontail and Western Scrub-jay nose to nose in what's left of a pie! While there was some fighting at the feeders/buffet, the animals all got along remarkably well. They do tend to share both their food and their space pretty easily. (This page) Here a Fox Squirrel, Western Scrub-jay and two Mountain Cottontails are all sharing nicely!

"I'm thankful for my health!
Nothing better than bright eyes and a shiny
coat- and I just got my new winter coat in!"

"I look shiny, too!"

Who you're seeing: a Mountain Cottontail and a Blue Jay- both looking quite healthy! It's always a joy to see healthy critters doing well.

"I'm thankful for apple peels! So glad you made a pie and had peels!"

"No need to peel mine! I just eat whatever falls off your tree! Whole!"

"Apples!"

Who you're seeing: (Opposite) A Western Scrub-jay and a Mule Deer. The Jays will take an entire peel slice and fly off with it! The Mule Deer are funnier, though. They pick up the apples whole and eat the whole thing- core and all- in a few big crunchy chomps! Many of the apples I used were from our own tree. We don't "feed" the deer, they just eat the apples that grow on trees. (This page, below) A Rock Squirrel, a type of ground squirrel, enjoys apples too! Love the stuffed cheeks!

"I'm thankful for a brave child who knows when to take a little risk!
Wow! How *did* you get up there, baby?"

"I just went up
the ramp,
Mom!"

Who you're seeing: (This page) A mother mountain cottontail and her baby. I don't often see the cottontails climbing things like tables. They tend to stay on the ground. This was quite the surprise! (Opposite, top) Three Black-billed Magpies squabbling on the table. (Opposite, bottom left) A Western Scrub-jay finding out that landing in flowers doesn't work too well! (Opposite, bottom right) A Scrub-jay and a Magpie fighting over a peanut. Their argument took them all around the yard chasing each other for fifteen minutes!

"Oops!
I think I took a risk trying to land here!"

"Me too!"

"Looks like I took a *big* risk
stealing his peanut. Yikes!"

"For peanuts... it's all about the peanuts"

Who you're seeing: (Opposite, top) A Western Scrub-jay with a whole in-shell peanut in his beak! (Opposite, bottom and this page, top) two Fox Squirrels. When I feed the birds, the Scrub-jays are the first to arrive when there are peanuts available! They'll keep returning until all the peanuts are gone! Interestingly, both Fox Squirrels and Scrub-Jays hide their food for later. I often see them burying peanuts and corn kernels!

"We're thankful for this incredible view!"

Who you're seeing: (This page) Two American Robins and a Northern Flicker taking in the early morning view of Pike's Peak. (Opposite, top) Nearby Blodgett Peak looking stunning in autumn colors shrouded by fog. (Opposite, bottom) A Fox Squirrel looking pretty against golden leaves.

"Me too!

Isn't fall

just so

beautiful?"

"Fall does have a special charm!"

Who you're seeing: (This page) Two female Mule Deer browsing the natural food sources in the neighborhood! (Opposite) A Mountain Cottontail. Both of these species are particularly well-camouflaged this time of year. It's easy to miss spotting them in the yard until they move!

"I just love cool, crisp days!"

"We're thankful…"

"For someone to love…"

"And I'm thankful..."

"For time to myself..."

"I'm thankful that my sweetheart, here, is doing okay"

"His left leg is broken and he can't walk on it... but I stick close by to help him out. "

Who you're seeing: (Both pages) My dear friend, Perry the Scrub-jay and his mate. When Perry first landed on the table, drooping one leg over the edge and just letting it hang, I was shocked. With an injury so severe, I couldn't believe how well he managed. But just like all the other jays, he comes and goes all day long, flying, landing, taking off, and hopping around on his one good leg. Sometimes he loses his balance and falls to one side, but he always gets back up. On the top picture on this page you can see his left leg dangling. In the bottom picture you can see that he eventually lost the leg. The day of this picture was the first day he arrived with just a stump. In watching wildlife you'll see many injuries, but that's part of life- even for us humans! Though we can all take a lesson from Perry: never give up, keep on going, and don't let anything get you down.

"Thank you so much for this!
Now we can store this food up for cold and snowy winter days!"

"I'm filling my
cheeks with **ALL**
the seeds!"

"Except for the seeds *I* can snatch up and hide for winter!"
"Whoosh!"

Who you're seeing: (This page, bottom) A Western Scrub-jay swooping in to grab some corn kernels and go bury them for later! Scrub-jays bury food for winter and have excellent memories to remember where! (Both pages) a Rock Squirrel with very stuffed cheeks loading up for the coming cold. (Opposite) A Fox Squirrel buries peanuts!

"Ha! Then I'd better run to unload my cheeks so I can refill! And I'll get Mrs. Rock Squirrel to come help me stock up!"

"Oops. I think I overstuffed these cheeks. I'm so full! I see why humans talk about a "Thanksgiving nap!"

"You goofball! No time for naps! Gotta bury the food...bury the food..."

"We're thankful..."

"For moments of complete silliness"

Who you're seeing: (Opposite, top) A Mountain Chickadee hanging upside down, chasing a dropped seed! (Opposite, bottom) A Rock Squirrel humorously flattened out on the table to get the last bits of corn off the cob. He kept pushing the corn, pinecones and pumpkins off the table...I was constantly running out to put them back up! (This page) A Western Scrub-jay balancing as it lands on a mini-pumpkin. I saw a lot of silliness while taking these pictures! And these three kinds of critters are some of the silliest. Chickadees are great acrobats and get in to all sorts of funny situations. Scrub-jays are both clever and goofy, and you just can't beat a Rock Squirrel's stuffed cheeks for a good laugh!

"We're so thankful for a drink of clean water! Thank you!"

"Oops! I'm trying not to fall right in!"

"There's even a rock here for tiny little me to stand on!"

"I love how the water sparkles."

"Swooping in for a drink!"

Who you're seeing: (Opposite) A Fox Squirrel and a Black-billed Magpie taking a drink. (This page, top) Two Lesser Goldfinches in the dish taking turns. (This page, center) A Western Scrub-jay peers in to the water before taking a drink. (This page, bottom) A Lesser Goldfinch lands gracefully with outstretched wings.

"Corn cobs!"

"I'm so thankful for corn cobs!!!"

Who you're seeing: (This page) A Fox Squirrel running off with a dried corn cob. Squirrels of all sorts just <u>love</u> corn! (Opposite, top and bottom left) A Western Scrub-jay holding down a corn cob to feast on the kernels. (Opposite, bottom right) A Rock Squirrel devouring a corn cob. He really wrestled the cobs and played with them!

"Silly squirrel! You're supposed to eat one kernel at a time!"

"How did that squirrel get this whole thing in her mouth?!"

"I don't know... but she has a great idea!"

"I'm thankful for beautiful mornings at sunrise..."

"And a nice buffet to wake up to!"

"And the way the sunlight glints off my wings!"

Who you're seeing: (Opposite) My little friend, Pumpkin the Mountain Cottontail. When I feed the animals in the morning, I often spot her sleeping under this tree, giving a big stretch and then coming to say hello- and to see what's on the menu that day! (This page, top) A Western Scrub-jay enjoys breakfast in the early morning. (This page, bottom) A Black-billed Magpie glistening in the morning sun. Aren't they beautiful? Can you spot the rainbow sheen on his tail?

Wait, wait! Pause the story... Susie speaking here!
I can't take pictures of this mess!
What have you guys done?

"Sorry, Susie! I guess we aren't used to this *fancy* dining!"

Oh, Mr. Rock squirrel, your manners are terrible!

Guys! We don't SIT in the dishes!!!

Oh, well... critters will be critters!

Who you're seeing: (Opposite, top) A Western Scrub-Jay in a messy plate. (Opposite, below) A mixed flock of House Finches, a Dark-eyed Junco and a Chipping Sparrow eating in the rain. You can see why I had to re-set the scene often! (This page, top) A Rock Squirrel, (This page, below) A Mountain Cottontail and a Fox Squirrel, all sitting in their plates! I would definitely say that the Scrub-jays and the Rock Squirrels were the messiest guests at the buffet- by far! As soon as they arrived the dishes became quite the mess.

"We're thankful for having great balance!"

"You show-off's! I've got balance, too!"

Who you're seeing: (This page, top) Two Black-capped Chickadees. They like to "hang" around a lot- literally! (This page, bottom) A Fox Squirrel running along a fence. They are well-known for their agility! (Opposite, top) a Lesser Goldfinch hanging from a thin rope. These birds are real acrobats! (Opposite, center, a Black-capped Chickadee on a mini-pumpkin. What a silly sight! (Opposite, below) a Western Scrub-jay on a gourd and a Fox Squirrel.

"Oh, my! This is not easy!"

"I feel somewhat ridiculous."

"Excuse me, I hate to interrupt this story again, but this dish is *not full!* It needs to be refilled!"

"We're way too casual to eat on that fancy tablecloth, so *the ground* needs to be refilled, too!"

"I'm having the same experience. Refill, please! I'm hungry for seconds!

"Oops! Another empty!

Who you're seeing: Some hungry little friends! (Opposite, top left) a Chipping Sparrow looking right at me! Opposite, top right) a Rock Squirrel with very full cheeks, who seems to still want more! (Opposite, bottom) a Dark-eyed Junco (Gray-headed race) and a Chipping Sparrow waiting on the ground. (This page, top) a Mountain Cottontail seeming to gesture for more, (This page, below) two male Red-winged Blackbirds (not yet with adult plumage)- also hungry!

"That's more like it!

Thank you for these full feeders! "

"Yes! *Thanks so very much* for thinking of us!"

"I eat on the ground instead of feeders, so I'm thankful that this *plate* is full!"

"So many full plates!

Wow!

You gave us such a great buffet!"

Who you're seeing: (Opposite, top) A Western Scrub-jay hanging precariously from a feeder. (Opposite, left) A Mountain Chickadee enjoying his lunch, (Opposite, right) Two Lesser Goldfinches and a House Finch enjoying Niger seed. (This page, top) a Dark-eyed Junco (Gray-headed race) feeding on the ground- as they are not fans of hanging feeders, and a Black-billed Magpie choosing from the full buffet.

"Thanks from everyone for doing this for us!"

"We're dancing for joy!"

"Happy Thanksgiving!"

"See you soon!"

"At the *next* holiday feast!"

About the making of Thanksgiving Pie

This fancy setup was just for show, just to add some color and elegance and whimsical fun!

Normally, the place we feed the wild birds and little animals is very simple and natural, like much of our yard! About half of our yard is left wild, with prickly pear cactus, yucca plants, many wildflowers, and other things that grow native to Southern Colorado.

After all, wild animals are just that- wild, and we want them to stay that way. We don't want to treat them like people because they're *not* people. But for a short time, they sure were funny to watch on tablecloths and fancy dishes!

The scene was re-set often to keep the tablecloth, plates, and water dish clean, both for better pictures and for the animals' health! The animals learned that if I was out there, fresh food was coming! So often they wouldn't wait for me to finish and would be scurrying and flapping nearby.

(Above) "Pumpkin" the Mountain Cottontail waiting just off of the tablecloth. I had shaken it out and she was waiting patiently for re-filled dishes! She often hopped around my feet while I was working. I've known her since she was a tiny baby, and she's one of my favorite critters who visits my yard! (Opposite) Two Lesser Goldfinches and a Mountain Chickadee take off upon hearing the camera "click".

This Western Scrub-jay never waited for me to finish setting up. He was always landing on the table or the feeder right above my head. I would hear him coming even before I saw him- as a loud "FLAP" always accompanied his arrival! I enjoyed his company a lot, even though he could be a bit noisy and pushy!

Yep, that's me! I actually sat on the kitchen counter taking pictures out the open window for over a month. My family put up with a lot for this book! My feet are in the sink, and they got wet often with two busy kids in the house!

One "problem" I faced was the fact that the "click" from the camera shutter scared the critters! The birds were especially startled by the sound, and in the beginning they would usually take off when they heard it. While this did spoil some really neat shots I was trying to get, it also accidentally provided me with a lot of great "in flight" pictures. It gave my feathered friends a chance to show off those beautiful wings! Eventually many of the animals came to completely ignore the "clicks" and just got on with their feasting.

Now it's your turn!
Create your own backyard habitat!

Feeding the backyard birds and critters is a hobby the whole family can truly enjoy. It connects us to nature, is immensely entertaining, and also benefits our wild friends. Many backyard songbirds are under great pressure to survive the difficulties posed by modern life, including pesticides, loss of natural habitat, pollution, and predation by domestic cats.

So if you're inspired to feed the wildlife, it's easy!

Our little friends really just need what we need: shelter, food, water... a place to call "home". But it can be hard for them these days, as many popular backyard plants, trees and shrubs do not provide good nesting or good nutrition! Whenever possible, try to choose plants for around your home that will benefit wildlife! Ask at your local nursery- they'll be happy to help. And consider xeriscaping- using plants that are native to your area- it not only benefits wildlife, these plants usually mean less cost to you in eliminated or reduced water, fertilizer and pesticide costs. Give it a try! We have many trees and shrubs in our yard that provide food for countless creatures- the bonus is it's a way of feeding them that's free for us!

A fresh source of water is always essential to a good backyard habitat, as are places to perch. Having trees near to any feeders provides great shelter, just make sure there are no good hiding places for predators to get too close! Make sure to provide good, high quality food for your friends and be sure to keep those feeders clean. You can find more information and advice at your local wild bird center, local library or online!

Get outside and enjoy nature!

You'll be amazed how relaxing the songs of birds can be- and how quickly you come to recognize them! You might also be impressed at how clever and interesting some of the animals you see are. Birds called Corvids, such as Jays, Crows, and the Magpies we have here in the southwest are highly intelligent and truly entertaining to watch. Squirrels, too, are known for their hilarious antics when trying to "break in" to bird feeders. They've turned out to be one of my favorite critters.

There is a growing movement stressing the importance of time outdoors- especially for children to have free, unstructured play time. With the stresses of modern life, many find that time in nature eases your frame of mind, relaxes your body, and rejuvenates the spirit! So get involved, and get outside! Spend time in nature with family, friends, and the wild critters and beautiful spaces all around us! There's so much to see and do. And most of all, enjoy yourself!

Our family just wanted to share our day of thanks with a little special "fancy" attention to our animal friends. And in the end, I think they enjoyed it as much as we did! And I hope you do, too!

-Susie Binkley

About the author

Susie Binkley is a writer living with her husband and two children in Southern Colorado. She has been an avid backyard birder and watcher of small backyard critters since childhood. Her enthusiasm for nature is poured into this book.

Susie's first book, *Squirrels in Deer Land: A Novel Celebrating those with ADHD, Giftedness, and other things that make us, well, squirrelly... ,* features wild critters as well, as all of the characters are animals! She is planning sequels to both *Squirrels in Deer Land* and *Thanksgiving Pie for the Animals.*

There are many wonderful resources for learning more about nature, including many great websites. These are *just a few* of my favorites!

- The Children and Nature Network (C&NN) has a wonderful site dedicated to getting kids outdoors: www.childrenandnature.org
- Richard Louv, co-founder and chairman of *C&NN:* wrote a bestselling book, *Last Child in the Woods: Saving our Children from Nature Deficit Disorder*: www.richardlouv.com
- The National Wildlife Federation (NWF) has extensive information on wildlife and backyard habitats, including ways kids can get involved: www.nwf.org
- For more information about backyard birds, including how to identify them, a good site to visit is the Cornell Lab of Ornithology website: www.allaboutbirds.org
- The Natural Resources Defense Council (NRDC) partnered with the Cornell Lab of Ornithology to create a fun site where bird lovers share stories, information and pictures: www.welovebirds.org
- A terrific resource on wildlife is the World Wildlife Fund (WWF): www.worldwildlife.org
- And to inspire you to get outdoors, check out the Sierra Club at: www.sierraclub.org
- And of course, don't forget the National Audubon Society: www.audubon.org

There are *so* many more- keep searching and learning!

www.ingramcontent.com/pod-product-compliance
Lightning Source LLC
Chambersburg PA
CBHW041504280526
45792CB00004B/1124